(Canada)

Fort Buford

Little Missouri River

BATTLE OF
KILLDEER
MOUNTAIN

Fort Lincoln

Fort Rice

Fort Yates

STANDING ROCK
INDIAN RESERVATION

Grand River

STANDING
ROCK AGENCY

MANY CACHES

GREAT SIOUX
RESERVATION

Cheyenne River

Fort Pierre

BLACK

HILLS

PINE RIDGE
INDIAN RESERVATION

BATTLE OF
WOUNDED KNEE

Fort Randall

Fort Robinson

Niobrara River

North Platte River

GREAT PLAINS

NEBRASKA

NORTH
DAKOTA

Red River

SOUTH
DAKOTA

Missouri River

MINNESOTA

IOWA

Map Legend

	battlefields
	forts
	goldfields

State borders reflect
today's boundaries.

N
W E
S

Above: Lakota tipis during a lightning storm. This village depicts how the Lakota traditionally lived prior to being moved onto reservations.

Opposite: A portrait of Sitting Bull, his mother (left), and his daughter Standing Holy, holding her child.

SITTING BULL

LAKOTA WARRIOR AND DEFENDER OF HIS PEOPLE

S. D. NELSON

Abrams Books for Young Readers • New York

Wakan Tanka . . . Wherever the sun, the moon, the earth, the four points of the wind, there you are always. —Sitting Bull

When I was a boy, I saw everything in this world as new and wondrous. Father Sun burned his bright circle in the blue expanse above. Sister Moon lit the night. Brother Hawk and Sister Meadowlark sang their sky song. The Cloud People rose into the heavens like white mountains cut deeply with canyons and gorges. Vast prairies of sweet-smelling grasses stretched beyond human sight. And Brother Buffalo grazed upon the earth in great numbers, like the many leaves on a tree that cannot be counted.

My band of people called ourselves the Hunkpapa. We were one of seven Lakota tribes that lived on the Great Plains of North America. Outsiders called all of us the Sioux. We believed that there is a living spirit in all creatures and things. We called this sacred spirit Wakan Tanka, or the Great Mystery. Into this land of mystery I was born.

At my birth, my father named me Jumping Badger. In my early boyhood, people nicknamed me Slow, because I seemed to pause in thought before acting. Later I would earn the name Sitting Bull—he who, like a mighty buffalo, would not back down.

The children of my village grew up laughing and playing. We boys ran footraces and shot arrows and threw spears at targets. Someday as warriors we would prove our worth in battle with these skills. Such games also taught us to be hunters. As men, if we didn't bring home meat, our people would starve and perish. From an early age, I sensed that I would be a strong warrior: My arrows flew more swiftly and true to their mark than those of the other boys. My weapons seemed to have a "medicine power" that gave me added strength.

The Great Spirit sent the buffalo. On hills, in plains and woods. So give me my bow . . . I go to kill the buffalo. —Lakota/Sioux song

In 1841, when I was ten years old, I killed my first buffalo. I galloped my horse alongside the young horned animal, loosing my arrows into his ribs. My pounding heart thrilled with excitement and fear. When the buffalo fell, I howled like a wolf in triumph. And yet, as I stood over the fallen creature, I also felt sadness deep inside me. I knelt close to my first kill and whispered into his ear, "Thank you, Brother Buffalo, for giving your life so that my people will live."

My Lakota people were warriors, feared and respected. We needed to be fierce in order to survive. We constantly struggled with other tribes over the use of hunting grounds. Our enemies—the Crow, the Pawnee, the Shoshone, the Rees, and others—were always trying to steal our horses. So we did the same to them.

In battles, I did what a warrior is supposed to do—earn honor through acts of courage. The bravest deed earned an eagle feather to wear in one's hair. This was a risky act called "counting coup." It was achieved by dashing into battle and striking an enemy warrior with a hand, a weapon, or a "coup stick," then escaping unharmed. The foe did not need to be killed. The daring warrior who counted coup first earned the most respect. Competition was intense.

At fourteen years of age, I earned my first eagle feather during a raid against our Crow enemy. On horseback, yelping and shrieking, I closed in on a mounted warrior and chopped him with my tomahawk. He fell from his horse, and another Lakota finished him off. Later that day, my father honored me with the shield and lance of a Lakota warrior. He also gave me a new, more honorable name—his name. Forever after I was known as Sitting Bull, symbolizing a powerful buffalo that holds his ground and never backs down.

A Sioux war party, c. 1880.

The whites go wherever they want to . . . Nothing can stop them. —Bear's Rib, a Hunkpapa Lakota chief

Many years before I was born, strangers began to come to our land. Their pale skin was curious, so we called them *wasichus*, or white men. At first they were few in number and said they only wanted to pass through the territory. They claimed they came in peace to trade for furs and buffalo robes. The wasichus offered amazing treasures and wondrous trinkets in exchange—horses, guns, wagons, kettles, knives, beautiful glass beads, coffee, sugar, and much more. Sometimes my people traded buffalo robes. Other times, we raided the wagons of the intruders and took what we wanted!

A wagon train of white settlers on the Oregon Trail in South Pass, Wyoming, 1852. The Oregon Trail, a 2,200-mile route that connected the Missouri River to the valleys of Oregon, passed through Lakota territory. The eastern section spanned part of the future states of Kansas, Nebraska, and Wyoming.

Soon the wasichus began to arrive in greater numbers, and we realized they had come to stay. They built trading posts. They made roads for their wagons and constructed army forts. Hundreds of their soldiers manned the forts. We called these soldiers bluecoats.

You are fools to make yourselves slaves to a piece of bacon fat, some hardtack, a little sugar and coffee. —Sitting Bull

The white men came to our land with two faces. They said one thing but did another. The trespassers spoke of peace and sharing while taking our hunting grounds. They slaughtered entire herds of buffalo—just for the animals' hides or simply for sport. The hide hunters did not view the buffalo as their brother. Instead, it was a *thing* to be used up and taken for profit. The skins were processed into leather goods, and the precious meat was left to rot. Their government leaders told us that they were the new owners of the land.

Before the white man came, thirty to sixty million bison roamed the plains of North America.

The United States government said that we Lakota must sign treaty papers that would allow their people safe passage through our land. In exchange, the government would give us rations of food—flour, bacon, sugar, and such. I refused to sign any treaties. We heard stories of terrible battles being fought between the U.S. soldiers and distant tribes. We were told that great forces were marching toward us. Their intention was the complete conquest of my people.

I took up my lance and led our people in many battles against the wasichus. Sometimes we were victorious, but other times we were not. In preparation to fight, we warriors always prayed to Wakan Tanka for strength. We tied feathers in our hair and painted our bodies and our horses for combat. We believed doing so gave us medicine power. Often I painted my face red and my body yellow. I painted my horse with lightning bolts and hailstones.

We must act with vindictive earnestness against the Sioux, even to their extermination, men, women, and children. —General William Tecumseh Sherman, U.S. Army, 1866

One summer, many bands of Lakota, my Hunkpapa people among them, were camped near the Little Missouri River at a place known to be good for hunting deer. Our gathering numbered in the thousands, including women and children. We had no idea that the wasi-chu soldiers were marching against us. They appeared in the distance as a blue mass of 2,000 battle-ready soldiers!

We fought in what became known as the Battle of Killdeer Mountain. The bluecoats opened fire with long-range rifles. We had only bows and arrows and old muskets we had received in trade. To our horror, the invaders unleashed exploding cannon shells upon us. We warriors counterattacked while our families fled in panic. Our men and their painted horses fell under a hailstorm of lead. We were overwhelmed and had no choice but to withdraw. The victorious soldiers destroyed our stores of food and burned all our tipis. We lost more than one hundred people in that fight. Only two bluecoats died.

> I want to know what you are doing traveling on this road. You scare all the buffalo away. I want to hunt on the place. I want you to turn back from here. If you don't, I will fight you again. —Sitting Bull

The U.S. Army won the Battle of Killdeer Mountain, but it takes many battles to win a war. I did not plan to surrender. Instead, I intended to teach the wasichus a lesson. Later that summer, I led an attack against a wagon train of white settlers heading west under military guard. On horseback and in close combat, I tried to push a soldier from his mount. He pulled his pistol and shot me through the hip. I was the one who learned a hard lesson. I lived, and my wound healed, but my warriors killed only eleven of the trespassers. One hundred of their wagons made it through.

Like a whirlwind, conflict and change swept into our lands. Some of us, including bands of Lakota, agreed to the U.S. treaties and gave up their hunting ways. They settled in designated areas near the army forts. They accepted rations and became what I considered loafers. I called them "Hang-Around-the-Forts." They depended on handouts and drank the white man's whiskey. It blurred their vision and made them stupid. They turned away from Wakan Tanka and bent their knees to liquor. Whiskey became their new god.

However, I refused to give up our way of life. For the sake of my people, I lived up to my name—Sitting Bull. I would not back down.

The signing of the Treaty of Fort Laramie by Lakota chiefs and U.S. officials, 1868.

[Chiefs] Red Cloud and Spotted Tail are rascals. They sold our country without the full consent of our people. —Sitting Bull

Time and again, the U.S. government sent leaders to negotiate with our people. However, we Lakota were very independent. We had seven tribes, or bands, each with its own chief and elders. We did not have *one* leader who represented *all* our different tribes.

The wasichus did not understand this. They picked Indians who favored their intentions and declared *them* to be chiefs. These so-called chiefs signed treaties, but they did not represent the will of all the Lakota people. This caused great conflict, because many Lakota refused to honor the treaties, and the U.S. government then claimed we were in the wrong. We were not wrong. We had not agreed to their invasion.

Although most Indians resisted the coming of the wasichus, in time many bent like a willow in the wind. Chief Red Cloud of the Oglala Lakota, Chief Gall of my Hunkpapa Lakota band, and Chief Spotted Tail of the Brulé Lakota all signed the Treaty of Fort Laramie in 1868 and surrendered our way of life. The agreement created the Great Sioux Reservation (in what is now South Dakota and Nebraska). On this reservation the U.S. government would teach my people a new way to live—to farm, to speak English, and to follow the ways of the Christian religion. In exchange, the chiefs promised to end the violent fighting among tribes and stop all raiding against white settlers. They agreed to allow settlers safe passage on wagon roads and new railroads to be built through what had once been Indian territory.

The railroad line that connected the east and west coasts of the country crossed through Lakota territory, as did wagon trains on the Oregon Trail. 1869.

One of Chief Red Cloud's warriors resisted and continued to live free on the prairies with a band of Oglala. His name was Crazy Horse. In battle, he painted a thunderbolt down his face and hailstones on his shoulders and chest. He fought like a thunderstorm. I liked that man.

I will do to the Americans as they have done
to me. It is not my wish to go to war, but I must.
I never told you before that I was a chief;
today I tell you I am one. —Sitting Bull

Leaders from our seven different bands agreed that we needed *one* leader to help unite our people against the wasichus. Many times these leaders had seen my success in battle. They had heard my songs of prayer to Wakan Tanka. They believed me to be a *Wichasha Wakan*, a holy man who would always put his people first and save them from destruction. A respected man named Four Horns turned to me and made the proclamation: "For your bravery on the battlefields and as the greatest warrior of our bands, we have elected you as our war chief, leader of the entire Sioux nation. When you tell us to fight, we shall fight; when you tell us to make peace, we shall make peace." Hundreds of Cheyenne and Arapaho joined us. Together, we would be strong—like a *herd* of buffalo that never backs down!

> # I am tired of being always on the watch for troops. My desire is to get my family where they can sleep without being continually in the expectation of an attack. —Red Horse

The treaties some Lakota had signed, hoping to improve their lot in life, seemed to make little difference. Again, the wasichus wore two faces. In 1874, a great army entered Paha Sapa—the Black Hills—which the treaties had set aside solely for the Lakota. The army was led by Lieutenant Colonel George Armstrong Custer—we called him Long Hair. The wasichus were looking for the yellow metal that made their hearts crazy with greed. Gold! It didn't matter that the gold was on Lakota land. Wasichus began to arrive in huge numbers.

Lieutenant Colonel George Armstrong Custer's base camp in the Black Hills, near where his men discovered gold, 1874.

George Armstrong Custer, 1865.

Alfred Terry, c. 1860.

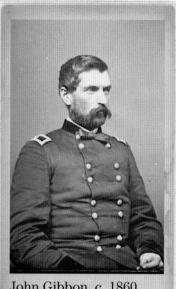

John Gibbon, c. 1860.

George Crook, c. 1870.

The onslaught of the white man continued like a hard rain that would never let up. The U.S. government demanded that all Lakota and Cheyenne report to agencies on the Great Sioux Reservation by January 31, 1876, in order to negotiate the sale of our Black Hills. Those who refused would be considered "hostile Indians." I knew that my people were headed for a showdown with the bluecoats. If the wasichus wanted a fight, we would give it to them.

In the spring of 1876, the U.S. Army launched a massive invasion of the Powder River valley (in the Montana and Dakota Territories), where my people and others were living. We were commanded to end all resistance and move to the Great Sioux Reservation. The soldiers had orders to surround and attack "hostiles" who did not comply. General Alfred Terry and Lieutenant Colonel Custer led 2,700 men westward from Fort Abraham Lincoln (in North Dakota). Colonel John Gibbon advanced eastward from Fort Ellis (in Montana) with 450 men. General George Crook approached from Fort Fetterman in the south (Wyoming) with more than 1,000 soldiers.

I will give my flesh and blood that I may conquer my enemies! —Lakota Sun Dance vow

That summer, when the sun was at its highest point overhead, I called for a gathering of all who were willing to stand and fight the wasichus. Hundreds of Cheyenne and Arapaho joined my people. My friend Chief Gall—leaving the reservation—and the fierce Oglala warrior Crazy Horse joined us too. Many frustrated Lakota who had moved to the reservation were not being given their promised food rations—they were starving. We warriors numbered in the thousands and were a force to be reckoned with. Together we feasted at our great encampment on Rosebud Creek. We traded war stories and celebrated. I called for the *Wiwang Wacipi*—the Sun Dance ceremony. Stouthearted warriors gathered in a circle around a cottonwood tree deemed to be the Tree of Life that grows at the center of the universe. The men pierced their chests and inserted skewers that were tethered with long cords to the sacred tree. Beneath Father Sun we lifted our eyes and prayed to Wakan Tanka in the old way of our ancestors.

I did not pierce or tether myself to the tree. My chest and back already bore many scars from previous Sun Dances. Instead, I offered up fifty cuttings of flesh from each arm and stood before the sacred tree all day and all night. A massive, moving circle of chanting people surrounded me. Their prayers seemed to hold me up. The next day, beneath the blazing sun, a vision came to me: Wakan Tanka would bless my people with victory. When I regained enough strength to speak, I told everyone of my vision: Hundreds of bluecoats would attack us, like so many grasshoppers falling from the sky into our village. But we would destroy them.

Is it wrong for me to love my own? . . . Because I am [Lakota]? Because I was born where my father lived? Because I would die for my people and my country? —Sitting Bull

As we continued to feast, Lakota scouts rode into camp, shouting that a great force of soldiers was advancing from the south, accompanied by more than 200 enemy Crow and Shoshone. Under the leadership of General George Crook, the soldiers pushed into the Rosebud Creek valley where we had gathered. My arms were so swollen that I could not join in the fight. Crazy Horse led our warriors in a daylong battle that routed Crook and his bluecoats. His entire army turned and retreated to the south.

Chief Red Cloud, c. 1880.

Chief Rain-in-the-Face, c. 1888.

Chief Crow King, c. 1880.

Chief Gall, 1881.

We moved to a new encampment on the Little Bighorn River. The green hillsides offered ample grazing for our enormous herd of horses. Late into the night, we celebrated our victory against the bluecoats at Rosebud Creek. Some asked if the battle was the fulfillment of my Sun Dance vision. Regretfully, I had to tell them that a greater assault was to come. Still, the feeling of victory filled everyone's heart. Our thundering drums and our deep-throated songs echoed through the valley.

The following morning, the gathering was quiet. Everyone lulled in the satisfaction of having won a battle. Most of the men still slept in their lodges. The women stirred and prepared meals at their cooking fires. The laughter of children and sounds of their playful splashing drifted up from the river.

I could whip all the Indians on the Continent with the 7th Cavalry. —George Armstrong Custer

Unknown to us, a force of 650 mounted troopers from the U.S. 7th Cavalry was advancing toward us. It was Custer, the one we called Long Hair! He had separated from General Terry's column of soldiers and intended a surprise attack from the south. Our hated enemies, the Crow and Rees, had joined him, serving as scouts. Colonel Gibbon joined forces with General Terry, and together they marched their army of 2,500 men up the Little Bighorn valley from the north. In the dim light before dawn, the Crow scouts spied part of our settlement on the Little Bighorn River. Most of our encampment was hidden by trees, but they could see hundreds of our horses grazing upon the hillsides. The scouts told Custer

to hold back, because they feared we were too many in number. They had no idea that we were more than 8,000 strong! Still, Long Hair was eager to win glory. He would not wait for General Terry's or Colonel Gibbon's enforcements to arrive from the opposite direction as planned. He would attack now, rout the Indians, and win victory for himself.

Suddenly, bullets ripped through the tops of tipis and clipped branches from the trees. I awoke to gunfire and screams. Above the melee, voices shouted, "They are charging! They are coming!" Like everyone else, I was taken by surprise. The bluecoats were upon us, just as in my Sun Dance vision. The soldiers were falling headlong into our camp like a dark cloud of grasshoppers! Shrieking women and children fell dead from flying bullets. I hurried my two wives, Four Robes and Seen by Her Nation, and our frantic children to a safe place and then mounted my horse. Every warrior grabbed his weapons and rode toward the invaders.

Hundreds of bluecoats were attacking! But we Lakota numbered in the thousands, and we were fighting for our lives. Chief Gall rallied our defense and led our men to drive back the first wave of attackers. Chiefs Crow King and Rain-in-the-Face, determined to fight to the death, led by their furious example. Our warriors killed many bluecoats and pushed them across the Little Bighorn River. I rode among the tipis, shouting encouragement: "Brave up, boys. It will be a hard time. Brave up!" As the people's chief, I directed all warriors toward the fight.

Crazy Horse led a force of warriors north and around to the east. They crossed the river and overwhelmed Custer's 7th Cavalry. The screaming horses, yelling men, and hail of bullets raged like a thunderstorm. Arrows filled the dust-choked air. The fearless Crazy Horse yelled out, "Ho-ka hey! It is a good day to fight! It is a good day to die! Strong hearts, brave hearts, to the front!" More than one thousand Lakota, Cheyenne, and Arapaho swarmed over the bluecoats like angry ants.

Warriors expect fierce combat. But it was wrong for Custer to attack a group including so many women and children. As our enraged fighters overwhelmed his, Long Hair realized too late that he had made a terrible mistake. Many Lakota believe that Custer saved one last bullet for himself; that would explain the hole in his left temple. He knew what awaited him if he fell into the hands of the people he had wronged!

Yes, just as in my vision, Custer's 7th Cavalry had come. And, like hundreds of grasshoppers, they fell headlong among us, and we destroyed them. But victory is not always followed by celebration. The war was not over. We learned that thousands of bluecoats were now advancing up the valley against us. We had no choice but to split up and retreat across the prairie. Crazy Horse fled with his band of Oglala in one direction. I escaped northward with my Hunkpapa to the nation of Canada to seek safe haven from the U.S. Army.

[Sitting Bull] is a man of somewhat short stature, but with a pleasant face, a mouth showing great determination, and a fine high forehead. When he smiled, which he often did, his face brightened up wonderfully. —Lieutenant Colonel Acheson G. Irvine, Canadian/British Assistant Commissioner of the North-West Mounted Police, 1877

My people lived in Canada for a few years. Our hunters managed to find some buffalo. But the great herds there also had been slaughtered. My people, their clothing in tatters, were starving and suffering from the long, cruel winters. The U.S. government told us they would provide food rations if we moved back to America, to the Standing Rock Agency on the Indian reservation. Desperate and dying, we had no choice. We surrendered our freedom and submitted to life on the reservation.

In 1881, I turned over my gun and my people at Fort Buford (in present-day North Dakota). I deliberately handed my rifle to my son Crow Foot. He then turned it over to the bluecoats.

Sitting Bull's son Crow Foot, c. 1885.

I surrender this rifle to you through my young son, whom I now desire to teach in this manner that he has become a friend of the Americans. I wish him to learn the habits of the whites and to be educated as their sons are educated. I wish it to be remembered that I was the last man of my tribe to surrender my rifle. This boy has given it to you, and he now wants to know how he is going to make a living. —Sitting Bull

A warrior I have been.
Now it is all over. A hard time I have.

—Sitting Bull's song after surrendering at Fort Buford, July 20, 1881

The soldiers put us on a steamboat and sent our little band of Hunkpapa down the Missouri River. I had never been on a steamboat before. The great machine had a fire burning in its belly and could go anywhere it wanted on the water. I was confounded—where did the wasichus get such power?

I had been told that we would join the Lakota who had already submitted to life at the Standing Rock Agency on the Indian reservation. But James McLaughlin, the agent in charge at Standing Rock, felt unnerved by my presence. Although we Lakota had no weapons, the U.S. government still feared me and my small band of about two hundred "hostiles." So, again the wasichus showed they had two faces. Instead of letting us join our people as promised, they sent us farther downriver and confined us at Fort Randall (in South Dakota) for the next two years. We received food rations and lived in a little village of tipis west of the fort. Soldiers kept guard over us. I had become the thing I loathed the most—a Hang-Around-the-Forts.

I have seen nothing that a white man has, houses or railways or clothing or food, that is as good as the right to move in the open country, and live in our own fashion.

—Sitting Bull, at Fort Randall

On the reservation, the Lakota were given plots of land to farm.

White Bull — Hunkpapa
Flying Hawk — Yanktonia

ttle Man — Ogallala
Dar Run — Oglala

Eventually we were released from Fort Randall and allowed to join our people at the Standing Rock Agency on the Indian reservation. Every two weeks we gathered at a storehouse to receive rations of flour, sugar, bacon, coffee, and other things. It was hardly enough. Once, my people had lived close to Mother Earth, and we supported ourselves as hunters. The U.S. government took our weapons and told us to become farmers. We had little choice in the matter, for the buffalo were all gone now. I was bewildered—how was it possible for the great herds to vanish in my lifetime? So my people plowed and planted. Seedlings sprouted. But the cruel summer winds tortured the crops.

I settled with my wives and children at a place called Many Caches—for the number of food-storage pits we dug there—on the banks of the Grand River (in South Dakota), not far from where I had been born. We lived in a square log cabin. I missed living inside the circle made by a staked tipi. I tried farming, but all my efforts failed. I raised chickens and some cattle.

The Lakota line up to receive food and other rations.

A famous American hunter, scout, soldier, and showman, Buffalo Bill Cody, invited me to join his Wild West show. I would travel to the east and elsewhere—the world the wasichus called "civilized." I had heard incredible stories about that world. I decided I would go see it for myself.

Sitting Bull and Buffalo Bill during the Wild West show tour, 1885.

People came by the thousands to see Buffalo Bill's Wild West show. They seemed to think I was the Indian who had personally killed Lieutenant Colonel George Armstrong Custer. I was booed with catcalls by some spectators, but cheered on by others. To them, I was a celebrity! Everyone wanted my autograph. It is strange to be both loved and hated at the very same time. Buffalo Bill and I became friends and traveled to many cities where crowds waited. As agreed, I stayed with Buffalo Bill Cody for one entire summer season. When I left, he gave me his favorite circus horse. The beautiful animal had been trained to do a trick during the loud gunfire at the end of each show. Upon hearing the blast, the big gray horse would rear back on his hind legs while kicking at the air with his front hooves. The trick always brought enthusiastic clapping from the crowds.

The gray horse rode the train with me back home to the Standing Rock Agency on the Indian reservation. My thoughts were confused with all I had seen and heard. My world had been turned on its head. How could my people adapt? I was an old man and tired.

Sometimes I would ride the gray circus horse on the prairie. Together we wandered here and there beneath the great blue sky. I prayed for answers. And the answer came. In the last days of summer, Sister Meadowlark sang her song. She sounded lovely, but her words were terrible and sad: *Your Lakota people will kill you.* My troubled heart did not understand. Everything in this new world now seemed to have two different faces—beautiful and cruel.

2 salt
3 sugar
1 bacon
1 salt
2 flour
1 coffee.
1 coffee
3 beads, red, white, blue
1 knife
1 beads, red

1 musket
1 powder
2 salt
1 bacon
2 yards cotton

1 knife
1 kettle

I will remain what I am until I die, a hunter, and when there are no buffalo or other game I will send my children to hunt and live on prairie mice, for where an Indian is shut up in one place his body becomes weak. —Sitting Bull

Some of our people still held out hope that we might one day return to our old hunting ways. In the winter of 1890, in a last-ditch effort, hundreds of Lakota gathered at different places across the reservation for the Ghost Dance—a new ritual to reunite the living with the spirits of the dead and to bring peace and prosperity. Many came to my little settlement on the Grand River. In their prayers and dancing, they appealed to Wakan Tanka. But their pounding drums and chilling songs terrified the wasichus, who feared there would be an Indian uprising.

I doubted that this new religious ritual had any true medicine power. Still, my people dreamed that Brother Buffalo would return to us and that life would be as it was in the old days. They believed that the Ghost Dance would bring back their dead relatives and that the wasichus would be overwhelmed and buried in the earth. I said little but stood by in support. It is wrong to tamper with the faith of others when they are near the end of things. Sometimes faith is all they have left.

The dancing went on for days. Many people gathered together to chant and pray. James McLaughlin, the agent in charge at Standing Rock, visited me. He claimed we both knew the religion was not real, so I should stop the dancing. But I knew his true reason for coming to me. He feared I would rally the people and stir things to a boiling point. That was not my plan, but he did not believe me, and he left.

In the dark hours before dawn, McLaughlin sent a small army of forty Lakota policemen to arrest me.

In the end, *my own people* came for me wearing the blue coats of American policemen. Can you believe it? Not only had they adopted the white man's clothing, but they had become a new kind of Indian. Perhaps they understood the way of things more than I did. Change was upon us, so they were changing.

I awakened to pounding on my cabin door. Familiar Lakota voices called out to me. "Sitting Bull, open up. We have come for you." In the early-morning darkness, they forced their way inside. They stuck a pistol in my back and pushed me out into the yard. They brought my gray horse, saddled and ready to go. From our little settlement of tipis and cabins, other Lakota awoke and joined the gathering. Anger began to stir in my heart. I pushed back and accused the policemen of having some nerve to come into my home in such a manner.

Uniformed Lakota police at Standing Rock Agency await inspection with their rifles and saddles.

Four Robes and Seen by Her Nation were there with our children. Hearing the commotion, more Lakota appeared to defend me. Heated arguing and pushing followed. A shot came from the crowd, and one of the Lakota bluecoats tumbled to the ground.

More flashes of gunfire erupted. In the gunfight that followed, I took one bullet in the ribs and another Lakota policeman put a bullet in my head. It ended for me that way. My handsome son Crow Foot and six members of my band fell dead with me. Another six Lakota policemen lay dying, along with two fallen horses.

He should have been buried in the old way—on a scaffold, safe from hungry wolves, in that high place reaching up to the stars of night. —Flying Cloud

Sitting Bull's two wives (Four Robes and Seen by Her Nation) and two daughters, outside their log cabin after Sitting Bull's death, 1890.

A traditional Lakota burial platform.

Some claim I was buried in one location, while others say my remains were taken elsewhere. In truth, no one knows where I sleep the long sleep. I should have been buried with my lance and my shield. But it makes little difference. What matters is that my people fought the good fight. We are not ashamed that we lost. We remain warriors, for the ways of the world are mysterious and fierce.

To my people I say: Brave up! There will be hard times ahead. Strong hearts to the front! Look, do you see? The buffalo are returning! Bury bitterness, for the wrongs of the past cannot be changed. Remember to honor those traditions that still serve our people. Share them with all who seek understanding. Go forth with a good heart.

In the end, everyone's spirit joins with the stars. Look for me there—riding my gray painted horse with feathers tied in his windblown mane.

SELECT TIME LINE

- **Late 1600s:** The Lakota Sioux are living in the woodlands of present-day Minnesota, where they travel on foot as hunters and gather wild rice, berries, and roots. The Chippewa/Ojibwa, who have acquired guns from French-Canadian fur traders, force the Lakota westward out of the forests and onto the Great Plains.

- **1776:** The Lakota push west of the Missouri River into Paha Sapa, the Black Hills, forcing out tribes previously residing in the area. The Lakota now claim Paha Sapa to be their hunting grounds, their sacred land, and the place of their origin.

- **Late 1700s–early 1800s:** The Lakota take up the gun and the horse. They create a unique nomadic (roaming) culture that follows the buffalo herds.

Statuary buttes in the Badlands of South Dakota. A typical landscape of the Indian territory.

- **1803:** The Louisiana Purchase. The U.S. government buys the vast expanse of land from the Mississippi River to the Rocky Mountains. Spain and then France, which previously claimed the land from the Native Americans, had not tried to settle it, as the Americans now plan to do.

- **1831:** Estimated to be the year Sitting Bull was born, somewhere in the Dakota Territory, perhaps at a place called Many Caches on the banks of the Grand River, which flows into the Missouri River in South Dakota.

- **1832:** The first steamboat travels up the Missouri River into the land of the Lakota Sioux. Many steamboats follow, creating an explosion in river travel and a boom in fur trading.

- **1840s:** Great Plains Native Americans supply 100,000 buffalo hides a year to fur traders in exchange for guns, tobacco, whiskey, glass beads, and other items.

- **1845:** "Manifest destiny" is declared to be a divine right by American political writer John L. O'Sullivan. He writes that it is "our manifest destiny to overspread the [North American] continent allotted by Providence [God] for the free development of our yearly multiplying millions."

- **1848:** Gold is discovered in California. In search of riches, tens of thousands of white emigrants begin crossing "Indian Territory" (land set aside by the U.S. government for the relocation of Native Americans).

- **1851:** The Treaty of Fort Laramie. A great treaty council is held between the U.S. government and the many tribes of the Great Plains at Fort Laramie in present-day Wyoming. Approximately 10,000 Native Americans from different tribes are gathered in the largest village of tipis ever assembled. An agreement is struck for Native Americans to allow white emigrants to pass unharmed through their lands. In exchange, the tribes will receive rations, clothing, and other goods for the next fifty years. Young Sitting Bull is present.

- **1854 (August 19):** The Grattan Fight occurs. The U.S. government does not provide the food and goods promised in the Treaty of Fort Laramie (1851), which set aside traditional tribal territories and ensured safe passage of white emigrants in the Gold Rush. Hungry Sioux steal and kill a cow from an emigrant wagon train. U.S. Cavalry officer Lieutenant John L. Grattan rides out from Fort Laramie and instigates a conflict in Chief Conquering Bear's village. The chief is shot, and the Lakota retaliate. Grattan's force of twenty-nine soldiers is killed. The press declares the fight a "massacre." The general public is put into an uproar and wants revenge. Thus begins the First Sioux War.

- **1855 (September 3):** The Blue Water Creek Battle (also known as the Battle of Ash Hollow) takes place. Six hundred U.S. soldiers attack a Lakota village of two hundred and fifty on the Platte River in present-day Nebraska, killing eighty-seven men, women, and children. The assault is led by Colonel William S. Harney, whom the Lakota call the "Mad Bear." He directs his troops to burn the village.

- **1861–62:** Native American tribes across the Great Plains attack and loot wagon trains and white settlements. These multiple conflicts between settlers and Native Americans result in the military engagement of the U.S. government against the Indians, and are referred to as the American Indian Wars.

- 1861–65: The Civil War between the Northern and Southern states moves the U.S. military's focus away from the conflict with Native Americans. At the war's end, the military returns its attention to the "Indian problem."

- 1862: Gold is discovered in Montana, and thousands of white emigrants flood into the area.

- 1862 (August 17): The Sioux Uprising (also known as the Dakota War of 1862) begins. The eastern band of Sioux had signed treaties with the U.S. government, giving up millions of acres of land for the promise of supplies. Meager rations arrived late or not at all. In desperation, starving, they attack white settlements and farms. They kill more than 700 American men, women, and children. "Governor Henry H. Sibley leads the counterattack with 1,600 Army soldiers and civilian volunteers. Within a month, he routed the Santee (Dakota/Sioux), taking hundreds of prisoners." At the resulting trial, 307 men are found guilty of murder and sentenced to hang. President Abraham Lincoln reduces the execution order, and 38 Dakota/Sioux men are hanged in Mankato, Minnesota, on December 28, 1862 (the largest mass public execution in U.S. history).

- 1863: Sitting Bull and his Hunkpapa band strike a temporary truce with the Arikara (sometimes called Rees) tribe living on a reservation adjacent to Fort Berthold, in present-day North Dakota. A disagreement over the outcome of a horse race stirs old resentments and nearly sparks a fight. An Arikara leader and Sitting Bull step in to settle the matter. Sitting Bull's leadership skills command the respect of his people and enemies alike.

- 1863–64: Major General John Pope orders Brigadier General Alfred Sully to establish several forts along the Missouri River and in the eastern Dakotas to secure routes to the goldfields and to eliminate the Sioux threat to the settlers east of the Missouri River.

- 1864 (July 28): The Battle of Killdeer Mountain takes place. As a part of the U.S. Army's 1864 offensive, Brigadier General Alfred Sully leads 2,200 mounted soldiers against the Lakota Sioux in present-day western North Dakota. The troopers have long-range rifles and artillery. Sitting Bull, being one of the war chiefs, helps lead hundreds of Lakota warriors against the attacking force. They are armed with outdated muskets and bows and arrows. Two of Sully's men are killed. It is estimated that the Lakota Sioux lose more than one hundred. Following orders from General Sully, several Lakotas' heads are cut off and mounted on spikes as a warning to other "hostile Indians."

- 1864 (September): Sitting Bull leads about one hundred Hunkpapa warriors against two wagons that are separated from their wagon train at Deep Creek, in present-day western North Dakota. Six U.S. soldiers and five emigrants are killed. Several Hunkpapa die.

- 1864 (November 29): Assured by promises of protection by the commander of Fort Lyon in Colorado, many of Cheyenne Chief Black Kettle's men leave their encampment nearby to hunt buffalo. Flying the American flag over their lodge to show they are friendly, they leave behind about seventy-five women, children, and males too old or young to hunt. U.S. Army Colonel John M. Chivington, who believes all "Indians" should be killed, tells his men, "Kill and scalp all, big and little." At dawn, seven hundred military volunteers attack Chief Black Kettle's encampment, killing and hideously mutilating the Cheyenne men, women, and children in what becomes known as the Sand Creek Massacre. The soldiers return triumphantly to Denver, Colorado, with scores of "trophy" Cheyenne scalps.

- 1866 (December 21): As American soldiers and civilians advance into the hunting grounds of the Lakota, Cheyenne, and Arapaho, Chief Red Cloud orders his warriors to lure a group of U.S. soldiers into a trap. Crazy Horse leads a force of Lakota and Cheyenne warriors, who, though armed with only bows and arrows, clubs, and spears, kill eighty-one Americans. In the last moments of the battle, which becomes known as the Fetterman Fight, Captain William J. Fetterman and his aides fear capture and torture and take their own lives. The Native Americans mutilate the dead soldiers but spare the body of a young, unarmed bugler who showed courage by battling with only his musical instrument.

- 1868: The Sioux City & Pacific railroad reaches the Dakota Territory, opening the way for more European-American settlement and transport.

- 1868 (April 29): Chief Gall of the Hunkpapa Lakota and Chief Red Cloud of the Oglala Lakota, among others, sign the Treaty of Fort Laramie, 1868. The treaty creates the Great Sioux Reservation, which encompasses the entire western half of present-day South Dakota (including Paha Sapa, the Black Hills). The U.S. government promises to issue rations and clothing for thirty years. It will also build schools and teach the "Indians" how to become self-sufficient farmers.

- 1868 (November 27): The Battle of the Washita River occurs when "Long Hair," Lieutenant Colonel George Armstrong Custer, leads a U.S. Army attack against Chief Black Kettle's sleeping Cheyenne village. More than one hundred men, women, and children are killed. The Cheyennes' horses (approximately eight hundred) are rounded up and shot. The Cheyenne now have no means of transportation or escape.

- 1869: Sitting Bull is named the supreme chief of the confederation of seven Lakota Sioux tribes.

- 1869 (May 10): The First Transcontinental Railroad is completed, linking the east and west coasts of the country. The influx of emigrants will be unprecedented and overwhelming.

- 1870: Chief Red Cloud leads a delegation of Native American leaders to negotiate with officials in Washington, DC. They travel from Wyoming on the Union Pacific Railroad. (Red Cloud signed the Treaty of Fort Laramie, 1868, sixteen months earlier. Congress ratified it.)

- 1873: The Northern Pacific Railway reaches the Missouri River at Bis-

marck, North Dakota, allowing greater emigration and transport of farm goods. Because of attacks on survey parties and construction crews, the railway company received protection from units of the U.S. Army.

- 1874: Lieutenant Colonel George Armstrong Custer leads an expedition of a thousand men into pine forests of the Paha Sapa, the Black Hills, where they discover gold. The trail they blaze becomes known by the Lakota as the "Thieves' Road." Within a year, thousands of miners enter the area in search of the precious metal. This gold rush violates the Treaty of Fort Laramie, 1851, which had promised the Sioux protection of their sacred land. Sioux warriors respond by randomly attacking the white intruders.

- 1875: U.S. Army General Philip Sheridan, appointed to pacify the Native Americans of the Great Plains after the war following the Sand Creek Massacre, states, "For the sake of lasting peace, let them [American hunters] kill, skin, and sell until the buffaloes are exterminated." It is estimated that within twenty years, fewer than one thousand buffalo remain in North America.

- 1875 (December 6): The U.S. government demands that all Lakota and Cheyenne report to agencies on the Great Sioux Reservation by January 31, 1876, in order to negotiate the sale of the Black Hills. Those who do not report will be considered "hostile," and the U.S. Army will march against them. Sitting Bull and Crazy Horse refuse the terms. Thousands of Lakota follow Sitting Bull, joined by hundreds of

Cheyenne and Arapaho. Others submit and go to the U.S. Army forts, where they are promised food and shelter.

- 1876 (May–June): The U.S. Army launches a massive, three-pronged invasion into the Powder River region of the Northern Great Plains against the "hostile Indians." General Alfred Terry and Lieutenant Colonel George Armstrong Custer advance westward from Fort Abraham Lincoln; Colonel John Gibbon advances eastward from Fort Ellis; and General George Crook approaches from Fort Fetterman, Wyoming, in the south.

- 1876 (June 4–8): Sitting Bull calls for the Sun Dance ceremony. After he prays to Wakan Tanka for a day and a night, beneath the sun a vision comes to him: hundreds of bluecoats falling into the Lakota encampment like many grasshoppers falling from the sky to their deaths.

One of Sitting Bull's daughters, Standing Holy.

- 1876 (June 17): The Battle of the Rosebud (also known as the Battle of Rosebud Creek) occurs. General George Crook's force is accompanied by 175 Crow and 86 Shoshone scouts (enemies of the Lakota). Crook dismounts his troops for a mid-morning break. A Lakota and Cheyenne force of approximately 1,000 surprises the napping army. Sitting Bull offers encouragement but cannot fight; his arms are too badly swollen from the offering he made at the Sun Dance. A daylong battle ensues. Lakota and Cheyenne casualties are estimated between 10 and 100. The bluecoats lose approximately 20 men, with many more wounded. Crook claims victory but withdraws his troops. He does not continue northward as ordered and is not present to support Custer at Little Bighorn eight days later. Thousands of Lakota and Cheyenne celebrate their victory over the next several nights.

- 1876 (June 25): The Battle of the Little Bighorn (also known as Custer's Last Stand) occurs eight days later in the Montana Territory. Lieutenant Colonel Custer and the 7th Cavalry attack the Lakota Sioux and Cheyenne at their encampment on a river they call the Greasy Grass Creek. It is one of the largest gatherings of Native Americans ever assembled on the Great Plains. There are more than 1,000 tipis, with approximately 8,000 people (more than 1,800 are warriors). Custer and his men are overwhelmed and killed. Sitting Bull is not in the actual fighting.

- 1877: European-Americans want justice and revenge for the Battle of the Little Bighorn. Thousands of U.S. soldiers mass on the Great Plains. Sitting Bull and his Hunkpapa band retreat to safety in Canada. Over the next few years, Sitting Bull sees his people suffer near starvation and exposure.
  Congress reneges on the 1868 Treaty of Fort Laramie and illegally reclaims the sacred Paha Sapa, the Black Hills.

- 1877 (September 5): Crazy Horse is killed resisting imprisonment at Fort Robinson, Nebraska.

- 1881 (July 20): Facing the starvation of his people, Sitting Bull returns his band of Hunkpapa Lakota from Canada to the United States and surrenders to the U.S. Army at Fort Buford, North Dakota. Fewer than 200 people remain in his band.

- 1881–83: Sitting Bull is held under house arrest at Fort Randall, South Dakota, for nearly two years.

- 1882: A congressional commission tries to pressure the Native Americans to divide up the Great Sioux Reservation into six small tracts and cede the remaining land for sale and settlement.

- 1883: Sitting Bull is allowed to go to the Standing Rock Agency in North Dakota.

- 1885: Sitting Bull joins William F. "Buffalo Bill" Cody's Wild West show.

- 1887: In the Dawes Act, Congress gives President Grover Cleveland authorization to divide up reservation lands and parcel them out to individual families. The individuals who accepted these land allotments would be granted citizenship in the United States. Any surplus land would be open for settlement.

- 1888: The Sioux Act breaks up the Great Sioux Reservation in present-day South Dakota into six smaller reservations. The remaining nine million acres are opened to settlers for fifty cents per acre.

- 1889: North Dakota and South Dakota declare statehood.

- 1890 (December 15): Sitting Bull is assassinated on the Indian reservation at the Standing Rock Agency.

Red Tomahawk, the Indian policeman who shot Sitting Bull.

- 1890 (December 29): The Battle of Wounded Knee, also referred to as the Massacre at Wounded Knee, takes place. In the middle of winter, the U.S. Army attacks the last wandering band of Lakota at their encampment in South Dakota. Under the withering fire of exploding artillery shells, 340 men, women, and children are killed. The defeated Lakota surrender. This is the last battle of the American Indian Wars, fought between white settlers and Native Americans over resources and territory. With the buffalo gone and the remaining tribes suffering starvation, the Native Americans move onto the reservations. The Lakota are now dependent on the U.S. government for rations.

AUTHOR'S NOTE

Cangleska Wakan, or Sacred Hoop: We Lakota people are still here. It has been written that the heart of our people was buried at Wounded Knee. Black Elk, the Oglala Wichasha Wakan, or holy man, said the sacred hoop of our people had been broken. He also told us that our people must walk in the world of the living, and the circle must be made whole again. It is bitterness over the past that must be buried—for the sake of our children. And, as Black Elk taught, it is up to us to mend the Cangleska Wakan of our tribes.

Sitting Bull's courageous spirit lives on in us. We are not merely victims of the past, and we refuse to sit on the sidelines blaming the long-dead ghosts of Columbus or Custer. With hope in our hearts, we move forward into action. We Lakota have a new story to tell. Like the people of all nations, it is up to us to define ourselves in the twenty-first century.

I am an enrolled member of the Standing Rock Sioux Tribe in the Dakotas. Although of mixed blood, I am a direct descendant of Sitting Bull's people, who were forced onto the reservation at the end of the nineteenth century. My given Lakota name is Mahpíya Kiŋy'Aŋ, or Flying Cloud. It is an honorable name that was also given to one of my great-uncles and one of my cousins. The name once belonged to my great-great-grandfather, a Lakota warrior. He was given the name because it was said that when he rode his horse across the prairie, the trail of stirred-up dust looked like a flying cloud. Twice he proved his valor by stealing horses from enemy tribes. His third horse-stealing raid against an enemy Crow village ended in his death. Mahpíya Kiŋy'Aŋ was shot full of arrows. The fighting was so furious that his body was never recovered.

The People of the Great Plains: *Sioux* is a collective term for three Northern Great Plains groups who share the Sioux language and a unique culture. These include the Lakota, Nakota, and Dakota. In turn, these three tribes are divided into smaller bands. The Lakota tribe included seven smaller bands: the Hunkpapa, Oglala, Miniconjou, Sans Arc (Those Who Hunt Without Bows), Brulé, Blackfeet, and the Two Kettles. Sitting Bull's Hunkpapa Lakota Sioux band was known as the "Head of the Circle."

Hero of the People: Sitting Bull, or Tatanka Iyotake, grew into manhood at precisely the right moment in history to experience the flourishing of the nomadic (roaming) horse culture on the Great Plains. Unfortunately, in his lifetime, the advancing European-American settlers would end his people's remarkable way of life. He was not born to royalty. Nor was he preordained to be the leader of his people. He rose to his position by courageous deeds as a warrior and by his sincere example as a man of prayer and loyalty to his family and tribe. Sitting Bull was a Wichasha Wakan, a holy man. He prayed and sought visions in order to gain insights and strength. He was a Sun Dance chief who led fellow warriors when they were pierced and tied to the sacred tree during the Wiwang Wacipi (Sun Dance). With a dignified manner of determination, he fiercely defended his people's traditional ways against the onslaught of the white man. Intent upon holding his ground, Sitting Bull was uncompromising in his negotiations with the U.S. government.

Sitting Bull's World and the Clash of Cultures: During the nineteenth century, two very different groups of people met on the Great Plains of the North American continent in what is called a clash of cultures. The meeting of these two war-like peoples resulted in battles whose names still linger in the vaulted sky above the prairies of the American West—Killdeer Mountain, Little Bighorn, and Wounded Knee.

Since the first Europeans had arrived in 1492, one group, the Anglo-Americans, were especially bent upon conquest. They had brought with them and continued to improve astonishing advances in weaponry, agriculture, animal husbandry, the sciences, mathematics, manufacturing, and steam-driven transportation. Their architects and engineers built cities connected by roads, bridges that crossed rivers, and ships that crossed oceans. Their written language enabled them to pass detailed information from one generation to the next. Driven by a belief in "manifest destiny"—what they considered to be the ordained right to take whatever they wanted—they claimed everything in their path.

The other group, the Native Americans, had lived on the continent for approximately 20,000 years. They were made up of many different tribes dispersed across the vast landscape. One group, known as the Sioux, was composed of numerous small bands of people who shared a common language and culture. Their way of life had changed little since the last Ice Age. As late as the 1660s, they were still, essentially, pedestrian (on foot) hunter-gatherers. Their tools and weapons consisted of chipped stone and wooden shafts bound together with animal sinew. The Lakota Sioux lived in lodges called tipis made of stacked poles covered with animal skins. No roads connected their small villages. There were no cities and no nation-states unified by a central government. They had not yet developed a written language. Concepts were passed from one generation to the next by word of mouth. Their only domesticated animal was the dog, which they rigged with a two-pole device called a travois for transporting belongings. The horse and the musket were introduced in the late seventeenth and early eighteenth centuries.

The Way of the Warrior: Originally, the Lakota Sioux lived in the woodlands of Minnesota, where, in addition to hunting, they cultivated small gardens of corn, beans, and squash. During the 1660s, their enemy, the Chippewa, acquired guns from French fur traders in the east. The Chippewa overpowered the Sioux, who still had only bows and arrows, and forced them westward onto the Great Plains. At the same time, tribes in the southwest had started trading horses acquired from the Spanish. The Lakota Sioux gave up farming and took up both the gun and the horse. By the late 1700s, they had transformed themselves into a unique horse culture that flourished for about one hundred years. With their newfound power, the Lakota became mounted nomads who followed the immense herds of buffalo across the Great Plains. Now a powerful warrior nation, they pushed aside other Native American tribes and claimed the Black Hills (Paha Sapa) and the surrounding hunting grounds for themselves.

Women in Lakota Society: Women were not hunters or warriors but tended the cooking fires, gathered water, put up the tipis, butchered the animals from the hunt, and tanned the hides. They were believed to possess "medicine power," for without women there could be no children. The women alone were responsible for raising the children. When the buffalo herds moved, and the people followed, the women packed each family's belongings. Horses and dogs dragged all the possessions, including lodge coverings, upon travois.

Traditionally, women were not allowed a public voice in the decision-making process of the tribe. Only men, like their counterparts in the wasichu culture, participated in council decisions. Among the Lakota, it was common, even expected, for a man to have more than one wife at a time. Having two or more women in a family helped divide the strenuous household chores. When a man wanted to take a woman for his wife, he was expected to bring an offering of gifts to her family. If the family thought the man to be strong and worthy, the gifts were accepted. In that way, without a ceremony, the warrior received a new wife. Sitting Bull had at least five wives in his lifetime and, according to some accounts, as many as nine.

The Nature of Truth: We Lakota believe that life is *wakan*, or sacred. The science of evolution has made clear what we have known since ancient times—that all living beings are related. We are all part of one family tree. Black Elk taught us that there is one truth. That truth has two faces. Both creation and destruction are fundamental dynamics of life. Order and chaos are intertwined in a dance of fierce beauty—this is a world of both curving flower petals and the sharp claws of conflict. We accept the paradoxical nature of life. The Judeo-Christian and Islamic traditions teach that God, the creator of all things, is only good, and that evil is not part of his creation. Yet evil is somehow created by human desire. In the Lakota worldview, the two forces are shared parts of the whole. In this mysterious dance of life, the warrior seeks to find a balance between the two opposing energies. Dealing with this duality is the challenge we all face. Life poses questions, and the answers are not always pleasing, or obvious. The honorable warrior seeks goodness for himself and his people. There is no devil in the world. But there are fabled troublemakers—Coyote the trickster and Iktomi the spider! Both are mischievous clowns who make us laugh or cry. As soon as we imagine that we are in harmony with the world, either one of these brats sneaks up and gives us a reality check. Like it or not, Coyote and Iktomi keep us on our toes.

Today, in the twenty-first century, many cultures fear change and cling desperately to the past. They use their traditions to build walls against the future and against their neighbors. We Lakota do not claim that our creation stories are facts. We retell our stories and myths to help us understand and adapt in this ever-changing world. Ancient rituals and ceremonies help us connect with the past and reach for the future. We sing our songs in order to remember our ancestors and celebrate this life.

For Lakota people, the Circle of Life is real. We see this fundamental truth reflected in the shape of Father Sun, Sister Moon, and Mother Earth. Even the shape of Sister Meadowlark's nest encircling its clutch of little round eggs offers this teaching. Love is round. Goodness is also round and wakan. We human beings are not at the top of some imagined pyramid with divinely granted dominion over lesser beasts. We two-legged beings journey in a circle with all our brothers—the four-legged, the winged ones, the green-growing beings, and even the little creepy-crawlies. In truth, we depend on all the living things in this world. In order to survive, we human beings must consume plants and animals—life must be taken so that we may live. It is only with this awareness that we learn humility and find balance in our journey of life.

ENDNOTES

page 2: "Wakan Tanka . . .": Utley, *Sitting Bull*, 144.

page 5: "The Great Spirit . . .": Schleichert, *Sitting Bull*, 20.

page 8: "The whites go . . .": Levering, *Annals of Iowa*, 1873.

page 10: "You are fools . . .": Marrin, *Sitting Bull and His World*, 92.

page 12: "We must act . . .": Dispatch to General Ulysses S. Grant, December 28, 1866, quoted in Marrin, *Sitting Bull and His World*, 92.

page 14: "I want to know . . .": Utley, *Sitting Bull*, 169.

page 16: "[Chiefs] Red Cloud and Spotted Tail . . .": Utley, *Sitting Bull*, 207.

page 18: "I will do to the Americans . . .": Utley, *Sitting Bull*, 205.

page 19: "For your bravery . . . make peace": Utley, *Sitting Bull*, 87.

page 20: "I am tired . . .": Utley, *Sitting Bull*, 181.

page 23: "I will give my flesh . . .": Marrin, *Sitting Bull and His World*, 39.

page 24: "Is it wrong for me to love . . .": W. F. Johnson, *Life of Sitting Bull and History of the Indian War of 1890–'91*, 201.

page 26: "I could whip all the Indians . . .": Ambrose, *Crazy Horse and Custer*, 435.

page 28: "Brave up, boys . . . Brave up": Vestal, *Sitting Bull*, 166.

page 28: "Ho-ka hey . . . to the front": Ambrose, *Crazy Horse and Custer*, 435.

page 30: "[Sitting Bull] is a man of . . .": Utley, *Sitting Bull*, 189.

page 31: "I surrender this rifle . . . make a living": Utley, *Sitting Bull*, 232.

page 32: "A warrior I have been . . .": Utley, *Sitting Bull*, 233.

page 34: "I have seen nothing . . .": Utley, *Sitting Bull*, 247.

page 40: "I will remain . . .": Utley, *Sitting Bull*, 206.

page 46: "He should have been buried . . .": Quote by S. D. Nelson.

page 48: 1845: "our manifest destiny . . . multiplying millions": Hietala, *Manifest Design*, 255.

page 49: 1862 (August 17): "Governor Henry H. Sibley leads . . . hundreds of prisoners": Marrin, *Sitting Bull and His World*, 75.

page 49: 1864 (November 29): "Kill and scalp . . . little": Editors of Time-Life Books, *War for the Plains*, 88.

page 50: 1875: "For the sake of . . . exterminated": Lehman, *Bloodshed at Little Bighorn*, 60

SELECT BIBLIOGRAPHY

Ambrose, Stephen E. *Crazy Horse and Custer: The Parallel Lives of Two American Warriors*. New York: Doubleday, 1975.

———, with Sam Abell. *Lewis & Clark: Voyage of Discovery*. Washington, DC: National Geographic Society, 1998.

Capps, Benjamin. *The Indians*. New York: Time-Life Books, 1973.

Catlin, George. *Letters and Notes on the North American Indians*. North Dighton, MA: JG Press, 1995.

Diamond, Jared. *Guns, Germs, and Steel: The Fates of Human Societies*. New York: W. W. Norton & Company, Inc., 1997.

Donovan, James. *A Terrible Glory: Custer and the Little Bighorn—the Last Great Battle of the American West*. New York: Back Bay Books/Little, Brown, and Company, 2008.

Editors of Time-Life Books. *The Buffalo Hunters*. Alexandria, VA: Time-Life Books, 1993.

———. *War for the Plains*. Alexandria, VA: Time-Life Books, 1994.

Ewers, John C. *The Blackfeet: Raiders on the Northwestern Plains*. Norman, OK: University of Oklahoma Press, 1958.

Hietala, Thomas R. *Manifest Design: American Exceptionalism and Empire*. New York: Cornell University Press, 2003.

Johnson, Dorothy M. *All the Buffalo Returning*. New York: Dodd, Mead & Company, 1979.

Johnson, Willis Fletcher. *Life of Sitting Bull and History of the Indian War of 1890–'91*. Philadelphia: Edgewood Publishing Co., 1891.

LaPointe, Ernie. *Sitting Bull: His Life and Legacy*. Layton, Utah: Gibbs Smith, 2009.

Larson, Robert W. *Red Cloud: Warrior-Statesman of the Lakota Sioux*. Norman, OK: University of Oklahoma Press, 1997.

Lehman, Tim. *Bloodshed at Little Bighorn: Sitting Bull, Custer, and the Destinies of Nations*. Baltimore, MD: Johns Hopkins University Press, 2010.

Levering, N. "Recollections of the Early Settlement of North-western Iowa." *Annals of Iowa* (July 1873), Greenwood, MO.

Marrin, Albert. *Sitting Bull and His World*. New York: Dutton, 2000.

Marshall, Joseph M. *The Day the World Ended at Little Bighorn: A Lakota History*. New York: Penguin Books, 2007.

———. *The Lakota Way: Stories and Lessons for Living*. New York: Viking Compass, 2001.

Neihardt, John G. *Black Elk Speaks: Being the Life Story of a Holy Man of the Oglala Sioux*. Lincoln, NE: University of Nebraska Press, 1961.

Schleichert, Elizabeth. *Sitting Bull: Sioux Leader*. Berkeley Heights, NJ: Enslow Publishers, 1997.

Thompson, Harry F., ed. *A New South Dakota History*. Sioux Falls, SD: Center for Western Studies, 2005.

Utley, Robert M. *Sitting Bull: The Life and Times of an American Patriot*. New York: Henry Holt and Company, 1993.

Vestal, Stanley. *Sitting Bull: Champion of the Sioux*. Boston: Houghton Mifflin, 1932.

Ward, Geoffrey C. *The West: An Illustrated History*. New York: Little, Brown and Company, 1996.

ACKNOWLEDGMENTS

I am grateful to Howard Reeves, Editor at Large, Abrams Books for Young Readers, for his dedication to the publication of multicultural children's books. His forward-looking intention helps ensure that our Native American voice will be heard in the twenty-first century.

Thanks to my friend Dakota Goodhouse—Ozúye Núŋpa (Two Wars)—at United Tribes Technical College in Bismarck, North Dakota, for impressing upon me the significance of the Battle of Killdeer Mountain, one of the great and terrible battles in the clash of cultures. I also honor his efforts to keep our Lakota/Sioux language and culture alive.

Finally, I am forever grateful to my brother, Colonel Terrence Jesse Nelson (U.S. Army)—Akíčhita Wašténu (Good Soldier)—for his queries and boundless encouragement of my writings and artwork.

IMAGE CREDITS

Endpaper facing the title page: "Sioux teepees in a line, North or South Dakota, during lightning storm, c. 1902." Photograph by Bennett Fiske. LC-USZ62-107576. Library of Congress Prints and Photographs Division. Page 1: "Portrait of Sitting Bull with Pipe, His Mother, and His Daughter Holding Child." SPC Plains Dakota BAE No #00500700. National Anthropological Archives, Smithsonian Institution. Page 6: "A Sioux War Party." Photograph by D. F. Barry. LC-USZ62-117638. Library of Congress Prints and Photographs Division. Page 8: "The Oregon Trail in South Pass, 1852." Photograph of painting by William Henry Jackson. LC-USZ62-51140. Library of Congress Prints and Photographs Division. Page 10: "Bison." Photograph by S. D. Nelson. Page 16: "General William T. Sherman and Commissioners in Council with Indian Chiefs at Fort Laramie, Wyoming." 111-SC-95986. National Archives. Page 17: "Special Train of Governor Stanford, president of the Central Pacific, and [wagon] train of immigrants bound for California at Monument Point . . . 1869." LC-USZ62-75148. Library of Congress Prints and Photographs Division. Page 20: "George Armstrong Custer's base camp at Hidden Wood Creek in the Black Hills, near where his men discovered gold. Photographed in 1874 by William H. Illingworth." 777-HQ-264-801. National Archives. Page 21: Custer, LC-B8172-1613; Terry, LC-BH83-142; Gibbon, LC-B8172-1464; Crook, LC-BH826-2600. Library of Congress Prints and Photographs Division. Page 24: Red Cloud, LC-USZ62-91032, Library of Congress Prints and Photographs Division; Rain-in-the-Face, photograph by D. F. Barry, B-156, Denver Public Library; Crow King, photograph by D. F. Barry, B-920, Denver Public Library; Gall, photograph by D. F. Barry, B-906, Denver Public Library. Page 30: "Crow Foot (Sitting Bull's Son)." Photograph by D. F. Barry. LC-USZ62-117643. Library of Congress Prints and Photographs Division. Page 34: "An industrious Sioux." Photograph by Frank Bennett Fiske. LC-USZ62-93149. Library of Congress Prints and Photographs Division. Page 35: "Ration Day at the Commissary." Photograph by Clarence Grant Morledge. RG2845 PH000008-000012. Nebraska State Historical Society. Page 37: "Sitting Bull and Buffalo Bill, 1885." Photograph by D. F. Barry. LC-USZ62-21207. Library of Congress Prints and Photographs Division. Page 42: "Police Force, Standing Rock Agency, N.D." Photograph by Frank Bennett Fiske. 1952-7773. State Historical Society of North Dakota. Page 46: Top: "Hunkpapa Dakota Women, Sitting Bull's two wives and two daughters, 1890." Photograph by D. F. Barry. 3195 H 2. National Anthropological Archives, Smithsonian Institution. Bottom: "A burial platform—Apsaroke," c. 1908. Photograph by Edward S. Curtis. LC-USZ62-46983. Library of Congress Prints and Photographs Division. Page 48: "Statuary buttes, Badlands, S.D." Photograph by J. A. Anderson. LC-USZ62-120380. Library of Congress Prints and Photographs Division. Page 50: "Standing Holy." Photograph by D. F. Barry. LC USZ62-117642. Library of Congress Prints and Photographs Division. Page 51: "Portrait of Red Tomahawk in Uniform." NAA INV 00515500. National Anthropological Archives, Smithsonian Institution. Back endpaper: "Ledger drawing, Sioux, Pine Ridge Agency, South Dakota." Drawing by White Wolf, c. 1884. MUSEUM OF THE ROCKIES/White Wolf.

INDEX

For the strong-hearted athletes
at Standing Rock High School—
Ho-ka hey! Lace up your shoes and get
in the game. Now is your time in the sun.

The illustrations in this book were made with ink and
colored pencil on 70 lb. paper, digitally placed on ledger paper.
This process was done digitally to ensure readability.

Library of Congress Cataloging-in-Publication Data
Nelson, S. D.
Sitting Bull : Lakota warrior and defender of his people / by S. D. Nelson.
pages cm
Audience: Ages 8–12.
ISBN 978-1-4197-0731-5 (hardcover) —
ISBN 978-1-61312-855-8 (ebook)
1. Sitting Bull, 1831-1890—Juvenile literature. 2. Dakota Indians—Juvenile
literature. 3. Hunkpapa Indians—Kings and rulers—Biography—Juvenile
literature. 4. Hunkpapa Indians—History—Juvenile literature. [1. Sitting
Bull, 1831-1890.] I. Title.
E99.D1N46 2015
978.004'9752440092—dc23
[B]
2014045761

Printed and bound in China
10 9 8 7

Abrams Books for Young Readers are available at special discounts when
purchased in quantity for premiums and promotions as well as fundraising
or educational use. Special editions can also be created to specification.
For details, contact specialsales@abramsbooks.com or the address below.

ABRAMS The Art of Books
195 Broadway, New York, NY 10007
abramsbooks.com

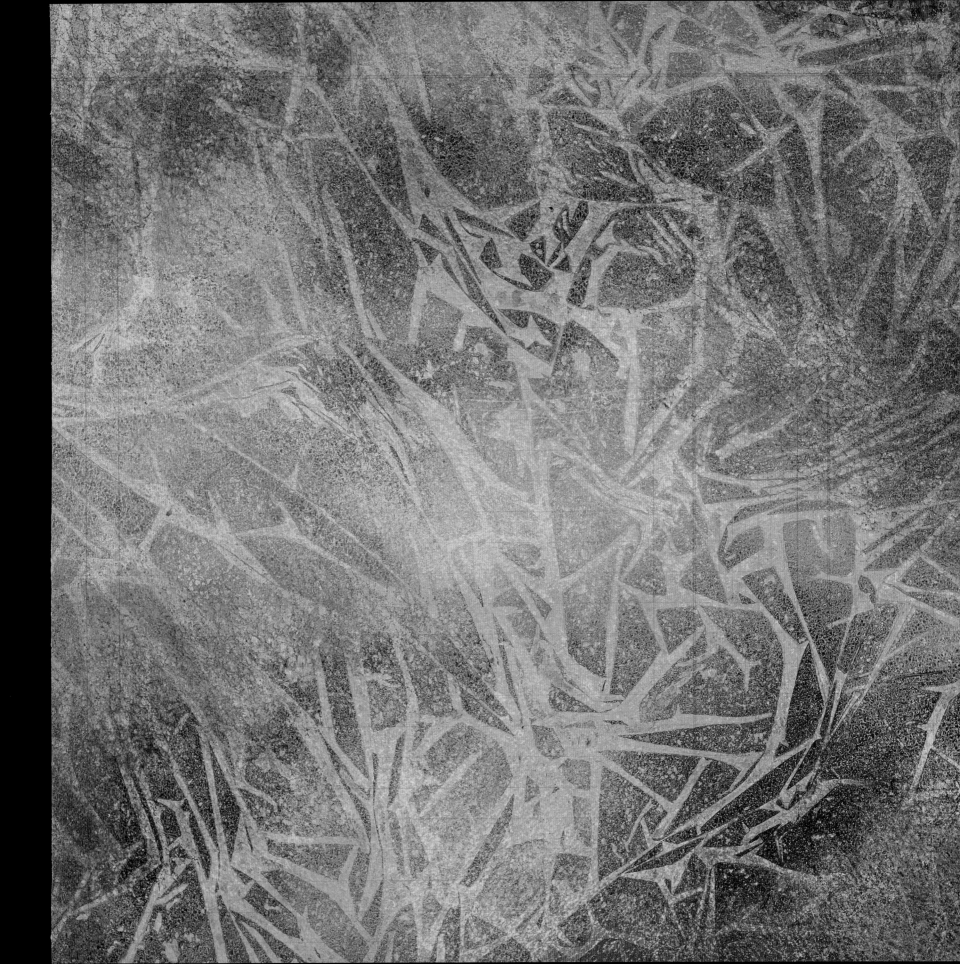

What Is Ledger Book Art?

A ledger book is a bound book with lined paper used to keep a sales record of merchandise.

During the last part of the nineteenth century, Native American people were forced onto reservations by the U.S. government. Some of the strongest resistance to this was among the Plains Indians. As a result, many of their leaders were confined under armed guard or put in prison. During their incarceration, some Indians were given discarded ledger books in which to draw.

The ledger books were "used," filled with numbers and written lists of merchandise. No longer of any use to the white man, typically they would have gone in the trash. The Indian artist was not deemed worthy of a clean piece of paper on which to draw.

Plains Indian artists had a long history of drawing and painting upon buffalo robes, clothing, tipis, their bodies, and even their horses! They quickly made the transition to working on paper. The artists used pencils, pens, and watercolors to create bold images of their vanishing culture, depicting village scenes, battles, ceremonials, and even their imprisonment. The stylized figures of people and horses are mostly drawn in profile. Ironically, and in a visually striking manner, the intentions of the book-keeper and the Indian artist remain separate—like oil on water. The Indian's images seem to float atop the lined paper of the "white man" with its strange written words and numbers. Sadly, and in the most compelling way, the two cultures never seem to connect. In many ways that disconnection continues today.

Art historians and art critics alike now regard the ledger book art of American Indians as extraordinary. The drawings are both historical documents that tell a people's story and works of art that stand as splendid visual testaments.

Ledger drawing, Sioux, Pine Ridge Agency, South Dakota, 1884. Depicts a Sioux giving chase to a bluecoat.